BACKPACKER

Peak Bagging

Brendan Leonard

FALCONGUIDES

GUILFORD, CONNECTICUT
HELENA, MONTANA

FALCONGUIDES ®

An imprint of Rowman & Littlefield
Falcon, FalconGuides, and Outfit Your Mind are registered trademarks of
Rowman & Littlefield.

Distributed by NATIONAL BOOK NETWORK

Copyright © 2015 by Rowman & Littlefield

All photos by the author unless otherwise indicated.

British Library Cataloguing-in-Publication Information available

Library of Congress Cataloging-in-Publication Data available

ISBN 978-1-4930-0976-3 (paperback)
ISBN 978-1-4930-1501-6 (e-book)

∞ ™ The paper used in this publication meets the minimum requirements of
American National Standard for Information Sciences—Permanence of Paper for
Printed Library Materials, ANSI/NISO Z39.48-1992.

The author and Rowman & Littlefield assume no liability for accidents
happening to, or injuries sustained by, readers who engage in the
activities described in this book.

Contents

Acknowledgments

My friend Tim McCall led me up Borah Peak in 2003, and the following fall when I told him I was working on my master's thesis at the University of Montana, he asked, "What's it on, peak bagging?" It wasn't, but I switched it to focus on peak bagging, and that may have made all the difference in my career. Tim accompanied me on every hike I wanted to do in the Missoula area that fall, including a hike up Grave Peak that we didn't finish until eight years later. I can't thank Tim enough for being a good friend during my two years in Montana, and for putting up with me when I knew absolutely nothing about the outdoors.

Outdoor Research has sponsored my adventures in the outdoors since 2011 and sponsored my writings at Semi-Rad.com since 2013. I've never been let down by their gear and apparel.

I've shared summits with dozens of friends and family members over the years and am grateful to have such amazing people in my life who want to have conversations while huffing and puffing up trails instead of sitting on a barstool.

Introduction

I went a little big on the first real mountain I ever summited: The easiest route up Idaho's Borah Peak gains 5,262 feet in 3.5 miles, all of it steep and none of it easy. I made a number of mistakes in preparing, the biggest one thinking that running a few laps around the local high school track every week would get me in shape for it. Turns out, there's a big difference between jogging on a flat track and climbing a mountain—about 5,262 feet of elevation gain, or 9,020 stairs, to be exact. It was a battle from the beginning, taking huge steps up the steep trail and talus and, of course, breathing at high altitude. It seemed kind of an odd thing to do for "fun" on a Saturday.

Still, at the summit, looking over the ridges of mountains to the west and the circular farm fields in the valley far below to the east, I knew I was hooked. Scrambling over the blocky southwest ridge with a few hundred feet of air on either side, crossing a short snowfield on the side of a mountain in late July, and never giving up despite wanting to every 90 seconds had made it the biggest—and best—thing I'd ever done in my life up until that point.

And the best thing about it is that there are hundreds more mountains to climb in the lower forty-eight alone. I got to work researching immediately, dreaming over maps and clicking photos on

Descending the ridge from the summit of Borah Peak, Idaho

SummitPost.com, 14ers.com, and other websites. What peaks were nearby, compelling, and within my novice ability? I was captivated, and the world outside my small Montana apartment suddenly became a giant playground I couldn't wait to explore.

After that first climb, I got in better shape, got some decent boots, and learned what kind of clothing I needed to avoid hypothermia and stay relatively comfortable in the big hills. In the dozen years since, I've never been disappointed with the view from a summit, anywhere. And I've managed to find myself on quite a few of them—from snow climbs in the Pacific Northwest, high ridges in the Colorado Rockies, and technical rock routes in the Alps—always dreaming of the next one within a few days of coming down.

ABOUT THIS BOOK

All who are drawn to the mountains find their own way to acquire the knowledge they need to stay safe and find success up high. I got lucky early on and met a few people who could teach me things about gear, weather, how to move on rock and snow, and, most important, how to be smart and safe about it.

This book is intended to introduce newcomers to the mountains, as well as provide a reference for more experienced hikers. There's a mountaineers' adage that has a few variations and has been attributed to several famous climbers (including Ed Viesturs, the first American to summit all fourteen 8,000-meter peaks), and it goes something like "Summiting is optional—coming home is mandatory."

This book will give you the tools to make it to the summit—and to know when to turn around and save a peak for another day.

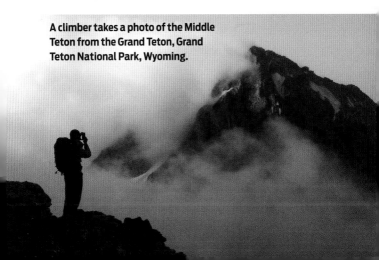

A climber takes a photo of the Middle Teton from the Grand Teton, Grand Teton National Park, Wyoming.

Chapter One

Introduction to Peak Bagging

In the hiking world, the term "peak bagger" has sometimes been used to describe someone whose outdoor exploration is motivated by summits—and, maybe in some cases a little unflatteringly, for people who have some form of "summit fever." I've always liked it and respected and admired many of the people I might consider peak baggers. I see them as self-motivated, people who aren't afraid to write down, or at least verbalize, their goals.

There are the folks who set out to climb all the Adirondack "46ers," all the White Mountains "4000ers," all the Colorado "14ers," or all the Colorado Centennial Peaks (the one hundred highest in the state) or join the Highpointers Club, whose members aim for all fifty state high points, from Alaska's 20,320-foot Denali all the way down to Florida's 340-foot Britton Hill, or the County Highpointers, who try to tag as many of America's 3,191 county high points as they can, from peaks in the Rocky Mountains to a particular surveyed

spot on a golf course in New York City. I say if a list of summits gets you into the outdoors, more power to you—you're lucky to have found something that ignites passion in you. Some of the best views in the world are from the tops of mountains—even better if, during the climbs to the tops of those mountains, you remember to stop and look around every once in a while.

Finding your way to a summit is one of the great joys of the outdoors, and it's important to know how to do it safely. As beautiful as the mountains are, they are completely indifferent to your success and your personal well-being. There's no lift to the top, no ski

Hikers near the summit of South Arapaho Peak, Colorado

patrol to call if you get lost, and no chalets where you can head inside and get a cup of hot chocolate when you get cold. The most important thing you should know about mountains is that they can kill you—even if you're just out for a day hike. Dozens of people have lost their lives on New Hampshire's Mount Washington when the weather changed suddenly and they were caught unprepared. Mount Washington is "only" 6,288 feet tall and has a paved road that goes all the way to the summit, yet it is one of the deadliest mountains in America because of something that's easy to forget when you start out at the parking lot and it's sunny and warm: the weather.

There are plenty of ways a good day out can go wrong: thunderstorms rolling in when you're on an exposed ridge, a loose rock accidentally kicked on a partner hiking below, a sprained ankle in loose talus, a fall while scrambling through a boulder field, even altitude sickness on a relatively low peak. Learning to mitigate these hazards is part of the game, and also why many of us head to the mountains in the first place: to learn self-sufficiency and accountability—and, of course, come back with some amazing photos.

With a few skills and some time in the mountains to practice those skills, your range of prospective peaks will only increase. Start on the peaks with well-maintained trails to their summits and work your way up to the scrambly Class 4 climbs and spring snow couloirs or winter ridges.

Chapter Two

Alpine Etiquette

In the mountains you are always a guest. No matter how "at home" you feel, one of the most important aspects of backcountry travel is to take only photographs and leave only footprints.

MINIMIZE YOUR IMPACT ON OTHER PEOPLE

Part of being a guest in the mountains is sharing it with other hikers—even if it doesn't feel like it at times. Just because you can't see other people doesn't mean they're not around. Never throw rocks off a summit. You never know if someone is hiking or climbing up below you, and the consequences of a rock hitting someone can be horrible, even deadly. In 2007 a hiker

Hikers on the trail to South Arapaho Peak, Colorado

threw a rock off the top of a cliff in Wyoming's Wind River Range, not knowing that Pete Absolon was climbing up the cliff below. After falling 300 feet, the 15-pound rock struck Absolon, killing him instantly.

When hiking, always yield the trail to users coming uphill. When they're coming up and you're going down, they're working way harder than you are, so find a safe spot to step off the trail and let them pass. Hopefully everyone will do the same for you the next time you're heading uphill. Every thoroughfare needs some sort of traffic rules or at least guidelines. Yielding to uphill hikers is the only trail traffic guideline in the mountains.

Be aware that during your wilderness experience, others are trying to enjoy the same thing: a little solitude. Excessive yelling, whooping, or yodeling on the trail or the summit might be fun for you, but it detracts from everyone else's experience out there. Chances are, they're looking for a quiet day in the mountains, not the feeling that they're in a sports bar full of noisy fans.

MINIMIZE YOUR IMPACT ON THE ENVIRONMENT

The mountain may seem like some giant indestructible thing, and in a lot of ways it is. But on a micro level, humans have to be careful to not have a negative impact. Multiply the effect of one person by a few hundred or thousand and it can take a larger negative toll on the places we love. You might think that no

A marmot ambles around the high alpine in Colorado.

one will notice if you leave a single candy bar wrapper next to a rock, but if every hiker thinks the same way, eventually the idea that "it's just a _____" will soon have the mountain looking more like the aftermath of a music festival than an inspiring peak.

Animals in the alpine environment have a tenuous existence in this very harsh place, and your interactions with them can interfere with their ability to survive. Although it might be fun to try to feed a marmot or pika, the wild animals in the mountains can learn to be dependent on food from hikers and lose the ability to find their own food. Once the hiking season is over and humans stop coming to feed them, their inability to find food can affect their survival. Equally important, human food can be harmful to wild animals.

A shrine of cairns near the Engelhoerner, Switzerland

Don't build unnecessary structures such as cairns or rock shelters. If the trail is hard to follow, a cairn can help, but generally, if you can see one cairn from where you're standing, you don't need to build another one. It's common to see a rock shelter on a peak summit, built for hikers to get out of the wind while they eat lunch or during emergencies, but the summit doesn't need to become a housing development. One such structure is usually enough.

Stay on trails when hiking. Shortcutting causes erosion, especially above 10,000 feet, where five footfalls in one day can kill a plant. Enough people shortcutting a switchback over the course of a hiking season can kill all the plant life anchoring the dirt in

It's important to stay on trails in the alpine environment.

place, making that part of the mountain susceptible to damaging erosion or washing out in a storm. Trying to shortcut a talus or scree field can be very dangerous if you step on a loose rock and send it tumbling down on someone below. When you encounter a puddle on a trail, do your best to jump over it (or just walk through it if you're wearing waterproof boots). Skirting it to the outside leads to the trail widening.

It should be obvious that you need to pick up your trash in the outdoors and not leave water bottles, food wrappers, and other items lying around when you leave. Although many people seem to think so, organic materials like orange and banana peels don't biodegrade quickly; they stick around long enough to be an eyesore for everyone else for years. If you packed in a piece of fruit, it's not that hard to pack out the peel.

If you want to give back as much as you get from being in the mountains, pick up trash when you see it, whether it's yours or not. A little maintenance goes a long way, and if other people don't see trash on the trail, they will be less likely to leave their own. Think of it as a way to thank the mountain for allowing you safe passage.

WASTE MANAGEMENT

Managing human waste is also important in the high country. Some management agencies require the use of "wag bags" or "blue bags," plastic bags used to carry out human waste on certain high-traffic peaks. It's not the most pleasant thing in the world, but you can imagine that if the 10,000 climbers who attempt Mount Rainier every year didn't use wag bags, the snowy peak would be a different color than white. And no one wants to imagine that.

When a wag bag isn't required, always bury human waste in a cathole at least 6 inches deep, and pack out all toilet paper. If animals dig up human waste, they'll often shred and scatter used toilet paper, so it's best to pack it out. Place a small amount of powdered bleach or laundry detergent in a small zip-lock bag and keep it in your pack for disposal of your used toilet paper. Never burn used toilet paper in the high country—it can easily start a forest fire in high, dry environments. If you're comfortable with the idea, learn to use

A privy with a view of Colorado's Longs Peak

rocks, sticks, and leaves for cleanup when you do your business. It might take a little getting used to, but lots of people agree that it's better than keeping a zip-lock bag full of used toilet paper in their pack all day.

When urinating, always urinate on rocks or dirt, not plants. High-altitude plants have a hard time staying alive in an unforgiving environment, and human urine can make them appetizing to animals. Alpine animals crave salt, and your urine contains salt. If you pee on plants, animals will eat those plants for the salt. In some areas, such as the Enchantments in Washington and on Mount Evans in Colorado, mountain goats have been known to stalk hikers, waiting for them to urinate—which can be a little unnerving, to say the least.

We're all guests in the mountains, and in the grand scheme of things, we're all just passing through. We owe it to all the people who follow us to the mountains months or years later to take care of those mountains so that others can have the same great experience.

Chapter Three
Equipment

John Muir spent most of his time in the mountains hiking with nothing but a stick and a sack lunch, so can't you do the same? Well, it's a free country. But lots of things have been invented since John Muir first wandered the Sierras, and if you want to try them, they're readily available. Chances are, they'll make your summit hikes a lot more pleasant.

Walking into a gear shop or large outdoor retail store can be a little overwhelming, especially if you don't know what you need—and you can spend a frightening amount of money in a very short time if you're not careful. Thankfully, peak bagging is one of the less gear-intensive backcountry pursuits when compared with sports like skiing and rock climbing. You only really need a few basic things to get started.

BACKPACK

What kind of pack is best for you? The most comfortable one! How big does it need to be? If you're only using it for single-day missions, you shouldn't need anything bigger than 30 liters and can probably fit all you need in a 20- to 25-liter model—unless you're planning on taking along some pretty bulky snacks and the entire Harry Potter series. At bare minimum,

get something with a
sternum strap and a
comfortable waist belt.
Your pack is going to
carry anywhere between
8 and 20 pounds of
weight; you don't want
that load pulling down
on your shoulders all day
and compressing your
spine. A well-fitting pack
with a solid waist belt
will transfer that load to
your hips, where it will be
much more comfortable.

A 26-liter day pack

What features do you need in a pack? It's easy
to get confused with all the options available in retail
stores today. Do you need pockets all over the outside? Not necessarily. You don't need immediate
access to much throughout the day besides food,
water, extra layers, your camera, and maybe sunscreen; and if you use a couple of stuff sacks to orga-
nize your stuff inside the pack, you don't need a ton
of external pockets. How about a rain cover? Rain
covers are handy, but just as good or even better in a
real rainstorm is the strategy of keeping your gear in
a trash bag inside your pack. (No water gets in, even
at the spots left open by a pack cover.) How about
a water bottle pocket on the outside of the pack? If

A backpack with too much stuff on the outside

you can reach the water bottle pocket yourself while wearing the pack, it's handy if you're going to carry water bottles rather than use a hydration bladder. If you can't reach the water bottle pocket while wearing the pack, it's not really that useful. Does the pack have straps to hold your trekking poles or ice ax when you're not using them? Your goal should be to have a pack that you can fit everything inside—despite what you might think when you see all the straps and loops and daisy chains on the outside of a lot of packs. The more stuff you tie or clip to the outside of your pack, the more stuff you have a chance of losing—and the heavier your load will be.

TREKKING POLES

Trekking poles run a spectrum, from old ski poles you can pick up for $5 at a garage sale or thrift store to top-of-the-line $200 carbon-fiber models that fold up to as small as 1 foot long. Whatever model you choose, they'll make you more efficient when you hike, and take some of the load (and impact) off your feet.

A hiker uses trekking poles on a trail in the Swiss Alps.

Lots of people say the poles take you from two-wheel to four-wheel drive, and on uneven terrain or stream crossings, they add a noticeable measure of stability.

How much you spend on a pair of trekking poles is up to you. The major benefits of more expensive poles are slightly lower weight and better packability. Think about when you want to stow your poles away so you can use your hands to scramble up a boulder field. Do you want minimalist poles that collapse to a size you can fit in your backpack, or are you OK with having full-length poles stick up above your head like antennae?

When buying trekking poles, make sure you get the right size: When you stand and hold trekking poles by the grips, your forearm should be perpendicular to the ground. Adjustable poles are nice if you want to be able to shorten them for steep uphills and lengthen them when going downhill.

HYDRATION

Do you want to carry water bottles or a hydration bladder? There are a few factors to consider, and which one you pick will largely be a matter of personal preference. Hydration reservoirs are convenient when it comes to drinking, and ideally you will sip water gradually throughout the day rather than chug it all at one sitting when you stop for breaks. Hydration reservoirs shrink in your pack as you drink throughout the day. A full 3-liter hydration reservoir is easy to keep in the proper spot in your pack—against your back, where the heaviest items should be. Keeping three 1-liter bottles packed in the right spot can be more difficult.

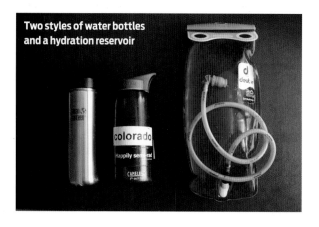

Two styles of water bottles and a hydration reservoir

Water bottles have their benefits too. They rarely leak. They're easy to refill at a stream crossing or in a lake (if you're carrying something to treat the water). You could fill one with electrolyte or energy drink mix and keep the other one or two bottles filled with just plain water. Inside your pack, water bottles rarely freeze; on a day when the temperature dips below freezing, hydration pack hoses can freeze solid.

WATER TREATMENT

During most single-day peak-bagging trips, most people will elect to carry all their drinking water instead of refilling water bottles from a stream or lake. But treating water can be a good strategy if you want to carry less weight in the mountains. If you'll encounter a lake once on the uphill climb and once on the descent, you can get away with carrying 1 liter of water and refilling the bottle once on your way up and once on your way down. One liter of water weighs approximately 2 pounds instead of the 6-pound load of 3 liters of water.

On overnight or multiday trips, you won't be able to carry all the water you'll need. You'll need to treat lake or stream water to make it safe for drinking and cooking.

Following are some popular water treatment options.

A hiker uses a pump-style water filter to treat drinking water.

Water Filters

Water filters are water treatment devices that remove pathogens including bacteria and protozoa, but not viruses. Removal of bacteria and protozoa is broadly considered to be sufficient in backcountry areas in the United States and Canada, less so in other areas of the world. Water filters have traditionally been pump-style devices but now include gravity filters, filtering water bottles, and filtering straws. The downside of pump-style and gravity filters is that they're slightly bulky and can clog in the field.

Water Purifiers

A water purifier is a device that removes pathogens including bacteria, protozoa, and viruses. Some purifiers are simply water filters with an additional step of chemical treatment to kill viruses, some are pumps that have more stringent filter systems and don't require chemicals, and some are ultraviolet (UV) water treatment devices. UV devices kill microorganisms with UV light. These lightweight devices run on batteries or are rechargeable and don't use any chemicals. The only downsides are that they don't remove sediment from water, and, because they're electrical, there's always the chance that batteries can run out in the field or they can malfunction (although most of today's devices are very reliable).

Halogens (Iodine or Chlorine Dioxide)

Iodine is a light, tried-and-true water treatment option. Most backcountry iodine users opt for small 1-inch-tall jars of tablets. The disadvantages of iodine are that it isn't effective against cryptosporidium, doesn't remove sediment from water, makes water taste like iodine, and requires waiting 30 minutes before drinking the water. Iodine is a great option to carry in case of emergency.

Chlorine dioxide works in the same manner as iodine but is slightly more expensive. Chlorine dioxide also requires 30 minutes to neutralize most pathogens, but unlike iodine, it neutralizes cryptosporidium (although it takes 4 hours).

Boiling

Boiling is the simplest, most effective way of treating water—there's a reason that during disasters, authorities advise everyone to boil water before drinking. The problem in the outdoors is that boiling drinking

A hiker downclimbs technical terrain to reach the descent trail.

water requires more fuel. It also requires setting up a stove and taking the time to boil the water, which can take a long time at higher altitudes. The extra fuel you have to carry to boil all your water on a trip is usually prohibitive to using boiling as a primary water treatment option. Still, it works in a pinch. There are different opinions on how long you have to boil water before it's drinkable—from 1 minute to 15 minutes—but as soon as it reaches a rolling boil, all the water in a pot is 212ºF or hotter and is safe to drink.

MAP AND COMPASS AND/OR GPS

There are plenty of ways to navigate in the mountains nowadays, including smartphone apps, Global Positioning System (GPS) units, and even the old-fashioned map and compass. Find one that you can competently use, and always carry it when you go out. Whatever method you choose, you should first learn basic navigation with a paper map and compass, because that's what all digital navigation tools are built off of—if you don't know how to read a paper topo map, a digital version isn't going to be of much help. If you choose a GPS for navigation, learn how it works before you take it on a summit hike. You don't want to be standing in a whiteout both lost and unable to figure out how to use your GPS.

PERSONAL LOCATOR BEACON OR SATELLITE MESSENGER

A variety of personal locator beacons and satellite messengers are now on the market, varying in cost from $150 to about $500, and are as light as a few ounces. If you're going to be hiking in an area with no cell phone service, they could save your hide if something goes really wrong and you're in a bona fide emergency.

EMERGENCY KIT

Hopefully you'll have a long career in the backcountry without anything ever going wrong, but it's wise to be prepared—just in case. I always carry a small stuff sack containing a few items to keep me alive in case I get lost, I break an ankle, or something else unforeseen goes wrong. My stuff sack includes the following:

» A space blanket—just in case I have to spend the night outside.

» A headlamp. I never plan to be caught out in the dark, but if night falls before I get back to the car, it's nice to be able to see the trail.

» A small knife. If you're lucky, you'll never cut anything but cheese and sausage with this, but it's useful for all sorts of things—from first aid to minor repairs to opening stubborn food packaging. I never go into the mountains without a small pocketknife.

» A lighter and/or waterproof matches. It's a lot easier to start a fire with these than by rubbing two sticks together.

» Iodine tablets—a small jar just in case I need more drinking water.

» A small first-aid kit (see below).

FIRST-AID KIT

Always carry a first-aid kit on your outdoor treks. You don't have to lug a big, total-coverage kit every time you go into the backcountry—it's only worth carrying the stuff you know how to use. At the bare minimum, carry a few adhesive bandages; tape; a small tweezers; antiseptic towelettes; a small amount of antibacterial ointment; something to suture wounds; and aspirin, acetaminophen, or ibuprofen.

ICE AX

If you're climbing on snow, you may need an ice ax. For most peak-bagging needs, a general mountaineering ax will do just fine. When buying (or borrowing) an ax, hold it by the head, with the pick pointing back and the adze pointing forward, and let it hang by your side while you stand. The spike should just about touch your ankle bone.

A properly fitted ice ax

HELMET

If a peak has a Class 3 or 4 section of climbing, rockfall from above might be an issue. If rockfall is a potential issue, rocks hitting you in the head at high speeds is a definite issue, and it's a good idea to wear a climbing helmet.

Chapter Four

Clothing

As the saying goes, "There's no bad weather, only bad clothing." You don't need the most expensive, newest gear in the world to climb mountains, but the first time you get caught in a thunderstorm while wearing a cotton T-shirt and jeans might be your last. Cotton kills up high. Once you sweat in it, it takes a long time to dry, and if you spend all morning climbing up and gaining elevation, you sweat. When you stop, the sweat on your cotton clothes cools very quickly, sapping your body heat and putting you at risk for hypothermia. Getting caught in the rain without a good shell can put you in a similarly bad situation.

A few key items can make your hike as comfortable—and safe—as possible. Of course not every hike requires every single item here, but it's a good basic list to start with when planning.

LAYERING

Rain Jacket/Pants

Don't plan for the best-case scenario, which is no rain. Weather will surprise you, so don't get caught with your metaphorical pants down. When it rains, at least have a rain jacket with you to keep yourself dry. Whether it's a $100 lightweight model or a $375

A hiker comfortable in shorts on a summer day in the Swiss Alps

top-of-the-line shell, "waterproof" is the key word. It's easy to find a solid rain jacket at any retailer, but figuring out which one is the most breathable and the most waterproof can make you feel that you need an advanced degree in physics or textile design.

In general, the more you spend, the more breathable the jacket will be while you're exerting yourself in the rain. You'll find a way to sweat under any rain jacket, from a cheap plastic poncho to the most advanced waterproof breathable material ever made, so worry about finding one that doesn't let in water from the outside—one that will keep your other layers dry in a rainstorm so you can stay warm. Rain pants might seem superfluous in the Rocky

Mountains and Sierras and on single-day missions, but they have more applications in wetter climates, where storms can last longer.

Soft Shell

A good lightweight soft shell jacket can be your best friend in the mountains, providing enough wind resistance to keep you warm during short breaks or while hiking through cold winds in exposed terrain. When picking out a soft shell for peak bagging, don't get something thick—think about moving in it. You want protection from the wind, but not a heavy jacket that's going to trap all your body heat and make you pour sweat every time you hike uphill in it. Many companies make great minimal soft shell jackets that both block wind and breathe well while you're exerting yourself. Find one you like, and feel free to use my personal test: Crumple it up in your hands after you try it on. It should pack down to about the size of a small cantaloupe. Any bigger, and it's probably going to be too hot.

Insulating Layers

There are traditionally two types of "puffy" jackets: down-filled and synthetic-filled. Several companies have developed jackets that combine down and synthetic insulation, but for the purposes of this book, we'll cover the two basic types.

Down is goose or duck down and provides the best warmth for its weight and bulk compared with synthetic insulation. The downside is that once down gets wet, it clumps, and its ability to insulate goes to zero. In dry climates like Colorado and California, this usually isn't a problem, especially during day hikes and short backpacking trips. You're not typically spending multiple days in a row hiking through rain or mist, or waiting out multiday storms inside a humid tent with lots of condensation dripping from the walls. Down jackets are more compressible, so they pack easier. For most day trips or short, spring-through-fall multiday peak bagging trips, a lighter weight "down sweater" is perfect. Many companies are now utilizing water-resistant down, which isn't waterproof but retains its insulating properties longer because it's treated with a water-resistant finish.

For multiday, cold-weather, or long snow climbs like Mount Rainier or Mount Shasta, where lots of travel takes place in the dark and cold early-morning hours, a stouter puffy jacket is a better choice.

Synthetic puffy jackets are a bit heavier and less compressible for their warmth but will retain their insulating properties when wet, so they're better for wet climates or during long mountaineering trips where things get wet and stay damp for several days at a time. They're also a good choice for days where you're doing a lot of strenuous activity in cold temperatures—snow climbs where you need that extra insulation but a down jacket is just too warm.

Either way, a puffy jacket is great to have along on a day climb or multiday trip—a warm cocoon to slip on over all your other layers on a windy summit, around camp in the evening, or while stopping for a quick snack on a chilly day. If you're hiking with a slower friend and have to stop a couple times throughout the day to wait for him or her to catch up, a puffy jacket can make those breaks far more pleasant and significantly increase your patience for your hiking partner.

Pants and/or Shorts

Pants or shorts? It's a matter of personal preference—and a dilemma made easier with the development of zip-off hiking pants, if that's more your thing. Shorts are cooler in summer heat because your legs can breathe, but at higher altitudes they can be troublesome because of all that exposed skin. Sunburn happens a lot more quickly above 10,000 feet, and exposed legs get cold quick when the weather turns or the wind starts whipping above tree line. Whether you choose shorts or pants, they should be made of synthetic materials (again, no cotton) that dry quickly.

Base Layers

The most important place to wear synthetic layers is against your skin—under all those jackets and pants. Wet layers on skin sap heat, so T-shirts, base layers, and underwear made of synthetic/quick-drying fabrics are important. Although you might love your vintage cotton "Stuyvesant Physical Ed Leader" T-shirt and can't imagine a summit photo in which you're

Two climbers descend a talus field below Colorado's Vestal Peak.

not wearing it, it's not a great idea—unless you pack an extra dry T-shirt to put on after that one gets all sweaty. But then you've got a wet, heavy shirt adding weight to your backpack.

A Note about Hoods

There's a saying, "No hood, no good." A hood keeps your head in the same space as your torso, which does wonders to help you retain body heat. You probably heard from your mother or a concerned elementary school teacher that you lose 90 percent of your body heat through the top of your head. That statistic comes from a slightly misinterpreted study about body temperature that makes it sound as though you can go outside wearing nothing but a stocking hat and be just fine. That's not correct, obviously. What is correct is that covering your head while covering the rest of your body keeps you much warmer than just covering your body. Jackets with hoods recirculate all the heat generated by your body, including your head, in one space. When you're buying jackets—rain shells, soft shells, or puffy jackets—get a hood if you want the jacket to be truly functional. I'm not shy about wearing multiple hooded layers at once—or multiple hoods at once.

Hats

A baseball cap or brimmed hat is a great thing to keep sun off your face and neck—much more important with the sun's increased intensity at higher altitudes. Remember that it has to stay on in the wind though—if a sudden gust pulls your hat off your head above tree line, there's a pretty good chance you're not getting it back. If you're planning on wearing a brimmed hat, make sure it has a string to keep it secured if the wind picks up.

A beanie can be worth more than its weight in warmth when the temperature drops up high. It's a good idea to always carry one in your hiking backpack when you're going up high, no matter what the weather forecast says.

FOOTWEAR

There are four main types of footwear for peak-bagging pursuits, and as footwear companies build better and more advanced shoes for the outdoors, the distinctions between the categories can get a little blurry. If you understand the basic types, though, you'll have a good idea of what to look for in a pair of shoes or boots for the mountains.

A Note about Waterproof Shoes

Waterproof always sounds like a better option, doesn't it? The pros are obvious (dry feet), and the cons seem minimal (a little more expensive, a little warmer in summer), so why not? In dry climates (the Rocky Mountain West, the Sierras), waterproof boots can feel like unnecessary expense and warmth about 90 percent of the time. But if you'll be crossing marshes, walking on grassy trails after rainstorms (all those wet grasses will drip water on your shoes as you walk through them), crossing snowfields, or crossing a lot of streams without bridges, waterproof shoes can be quite nice. But remember: A 3-inch-high waterproof shoe (e.g., a trail running shoe or approach shoe) is only waterproof up to 3 inches.

Hiking Boots

The tried-and-true standby of hikers and backpackers, hiking boots deliver stability, ankle protection, and sturdy foot coverage. High-top and mid-height boots give hikers confidence on uneven terrain, and if you're the type to roll or sprain an ankle, they're probably the best choice for peak bagging. The downside when compared with low-top shoes is their heavier weight—a few extra ounces on your

Women's mountaineering boots, approach shoes, trail running shoes

feet can feel like a lot when you're taking thousands of steps in a day.

Mountaineering Boots

The slightly sturdier cousin of hiking boots, mountaineering boots have a full or three-quarter shank in the midsole, making the sole stiff so that you can strap a crampon to the boot and it won't pop off. A stiff sole may sound uncomfortable compared with a hiking boot sole, but mountaineering boots usually have a rocker sole—a slightly curved profile that allows the foot to roll through steps. If you plan on doing some snow climbing or need a very stiff sole to protect sensitive feet, mountaineering boots are a great choice. For most purposes, three-season mountaineering boots are the best choice; winter mountaineering boots will be too heavy and too hot.

Approach Shoes

First developed for rock climbers who need to scramble over rocks and slabs on their way to climbing areas or routes, approach shoes have a stickier rubber on the outsole of the forefoot (or entire foot), making them more secure when smearing on rock surfaces. Some are designed more like trail running shoes, and some are more like light hikers, but most models are low-top shoes. If you're doing a lot of scrambling on talus or just a lot of hiking on rocks above tree line and don't feel that you need ankle support, approach shoes can be a great choice.

Trail Running Shoes

Trail running shoes are usually the most lightweight and comfortable option for hiking, and plenty of outdoor enthusiasts don't wear anything else. If you have sturdy ankles, want to go light (and theoretically fast), and don't need a stiff sole or sturdy uppers to defend your feet from rocks and roots, trail running shoes are a great choice. As previously mentioned, companies are developing shoes that blur the lines among all the categories, and there are definitely burly trail running shoes with sticky rubber outsoles out there.

Socks

Most sock options are synthetic, wool, or a blend of the two. The thickness is up to you; there's no reason other than personal preference to recommend something thick or thin. You'll know very soon if the socks you've chosen to wear with your boots or shoes are the right ones—or if you're getting blisters because your socks are too thick or too thin.

One thing to consider with hiking or mountaineering boots: Many people like to wear a "liner sock" underneath another sock in boots. Boots are generally a little less flexible than shoes, and a liner sock provides another layer between your skin and any hot spots on the inside of the boot. Your first sock will rub against the liner sock instead of making a blister somewhere on your foot.

Gaiters

Should you wear gaiters? If you're going to encounter some snow on your hike, gaiters can mean the difference between soaking wet, cold feet and comfy, dry feet. On Mount Rainier or Mount Hood, for instance, they're probably a good idea, but on a peak where there's only a small snowfield, they're probably overkill. If you expect only a moderate amount of snow, here's something else to consider: Lots of apparel companies have built grommets or hooks onto the cuffs of their climbing and hiking pants. You can attach a short piece of 2- or 3-millimeter cord to the pants and clip the cord under the arch of your boots— your pants will stay securely down around your shoes and keep snow out of them. That little piece of cord is very lightweight compared to a pair of gaiters.

Chapter Five

Weather

You don't need to be a meteorologist to stay safe in the mountains (although it might be nice). The main thing to realize about weather is that it's one of the most dangerous parts of an alpine environment. You should respect it and make prudent decisions with that respect in mind. Knowing the differences between different types of clouds is far less important than knowing when to turn around and head back down because clouds are gathering nearby. Being thoughtful about a few key weather elements can keep you safe up high.

TEMPERATURES

One of the most popular adages about weather is "Don't like the weather around here? Wait a minute—it'll change." Nowhere is this truer than in the mountains. If you've spent any time at higher elevations or above tree line, you might have noticed that you can never quite figure out what layers you need to have on. You're cold, so you put on a jacket; then the sun comes out and you're hot, so you take the jacket off. Then you round a corner and feel a cool breeze. In a few minutes you're freezing again, so you have to stop and put the jacket back on.

Two climbers descend a technical gully on Colorado's Mt. Neva.

Temperatures can swing wildly in the mountains; even on a day hike they can vary greatly from the trailhead to the summit. A good rule of thumb is that for each 1,000 feet you climb up, the temperature drops three degrees Fahrenheit. So if the weather forecast is for a high of 70ºF in Denver, elevation

5,280 feet, the high temperature on the summit of nearby Grays Peak, elevation 14,278, will be closer to 43°F—probably even lower because it's totally exposed to the wind. Pack your pack accordingly, and remember to "start cold." When you're hiking uphill, your body temperature rises quickly, so start from the trailhead in as few layers as possible. If you're comfortable standing in a jacket at the trailhead, you'll probably be sweating a few hundred feet up the trail. So pack away the jacket before you start; conserve those body fluids, and avoid having a sweat-soaked back (and backpack), which will be really cold once you hit the breeze up high.

CLOUDS

We'd love to have every day in the mountains be a "bluebird" day, but of course that rarely happens. Clouds will form, and reading them is an entire science on its own. The important thing is to watch them while you're on your way up a peak. Lots of cumulus clouds (tall puffy clouds that look like cotton balls), even if they're not that close, can build quickly into cumulonimbus clouds, which can produce storms—and you don't want to be on a mountain in a thunderstorm, for multiple reasons (see below). A few clouds on the horizon is no reason to abandon your plans for the day, but keep an eye on the clouds. If they're getting darker, looking a little more threatening, or building

Storm clouds roll in over Colorado's Indian Peaks.

into towering cumulonimbus clouds, it's probably time to call it a day and come back another time.

PRECIPITATION

It's true that you're not going to melt in the rain. But it can cause some other problems, and moisture up high is of a bit more consequence than it is when you're just walking home from the grocery store.

If you're caught in a lot of rain and get soaked (not that the jacket leaks, but the outer layer of the shell will absorb water, which will feel cold), you can be at risk for hypothermia, especially if all your layers are soaked too and you're a long way from the trailhead.

If you're on a peak and a cloud moves in on top of you, compromising your visibility, navigating can be difficult. A talus field you just scrambled up can look a lot different on the way down, and more than one climbing disaster has begun with a person getting lost in a jumble of rocks.

Moisture on rocks obviously makes them slippery, both under your hiking shoes and on one another. When scrambling through a talus field after rain, be extra careful about slipping on boulders and the boulders themselves shifting.

Even when the air temperature doesn't feel that cold, a stiff breeze during a moisture event can freeze a small amount of water on rocks, creating a thin layer of verglas, or thin ice. Verglas usually looks just like water but, as you might guess, is a lot more slick—which you might not notice until your foot slips on it.

LIGHTNING

Mountaintops are one of the least desirable places to be during a thunderstorm—you're exposed, usually closer to the storm because you're at high elevation, and often far from being able to get to cover below tree line. Lightning-detection equipment has confirmed strikes up to 50 miles away from a parent thunderstorm, but it usually travels 10 miles or less. Still, a black cloud 10 miles away when you're on a mountainside is an unnerving thing, and when you hear rumbles of thunder or see clouds building into a storm, it's best to play it safe: Turn around and head back down.

To minimize your chances of getting caught in a storm, get an early start on your climb. In high-elevation areas, plan to be on the summit and heading down by noon, if not earlier; thunderstorms usually happen in the afternoon hours but can occur anytime, so always pay attention to clouds building. When you estimate how long a particular hike is going to take, it doesn't hurt to add 30 minutes to 1 hour to your time frame. You're almost never as fast as you think you'll be, especially when you add in some bathroom breaks and layering and de-layering as you head up. Figure in your driving time to the trailhead as well, and add more time if you'll be driving a few miles on a bumpy dirt road to get to the trailhead, because you likely won't be going 65 mph. Don't be shy about getting an "alpine start"—this is mountain climbing, not brunch, after all. I've started long days in the mountains as early as 1:30 a.m. from my Denver apartment. I've been surly getting out of bed but never disappointed watching the sun rise from the trail—or being safe back at the trailhead when the thunder and rain started coming down.

If you are caught in a storm, do your best to get below tree line. If you can't get below tree line and the storm is right on top of you, get into lightning position: Take off your pack, stand on it, then squat down and hug your knees. If your trekking poles are metal or you have an ice ax on your pack, get them away from you.

WHEN TO BAIL

There is no magic equation to add up weather elements and decide that today's just not your day in the mountains. As a friend said once at a windy trailhead, "I'm not worried about it being unsafe. I'm worried about it not being fun." Whether or not it's safe should always be your number-one concern.

If you have proper gear and clothing for the elements, you can often tough out a period of unstable weather. Maybe the rain will only last 30 minutes and the storm will pass over while you wait in the trees. There's certainly no harm in starting out and seeing what happens as you make your way up the trail—conditions might improve.

But always be aware that you can't will good weather. Just because you want to get to the top of a mountain today doesn't mean the weather will cooperate. Sure, you want to get that summit, but you don't want to be that person who had to get rescued off the mountain—or worse—because you made a bunch of bad decisions.

Clouds sock in a high ridge, decreasing visibility to 150 feet.

Chapter Six
On the Trail

Once you've got an objective picked out, all your gear organized, and hopefully a friend to go along with you, all that's left is the fun part: heading for the summit—and taking some photos.

KNOW WHERE YOU'RE GOING

Before you head out on a summit hike, figure out where you're going. As simple as it may sound, all kinds of people do get lost—including people who do not believe they're lost or believe they can ever get lost (men, I'm looking at you/us). When you pick a peak to climb for the first time, it's your first time in a new place; and as much as you'd like to believe you have an intrinsic sense of direction or wilderness navigation, it's a good idea to seek out some information beforehand. A wrong turn at a trail junction or an error in route finding can cost minutes, or hours, and be the difference between standing on the summit and wandering around in the woods.

Before you go, do a quick Internet search for information. Trip reports, hiking blogs, and other websites can provide tons of beta on your hike, and the information can be more current (or even more accurate) than guidebooks—when a trail is snow-free, if a

Checking out the map at home before heading out on a trip

bridge has washed out, whether the road to the trail-head is passable in a non-four-wheel-drive vehicle, if there's camping nearby, if there are water sources to refill water bottles and if those sources have water year-round, and more.

Get a map, even if it's an online topo map, and review it beforehand, even if you think it's the most straightforward hike in the world and only an idiot would get lost—because you don't want to be that idiot. Consider the mileage, and especially consider the elevation gain from the trailhead to the summit. Think about how long it will take you to complete the hike. Six miles of flat city running is a lot different than a 6-mile hike in the mountains. You may be able to cover 1,000 vertical feet in 1 hour, but what about when you get above 12,000 feet? You might (and probably will) slow down considerably. Will you be moving on a good trail the entire time or scrambling? That will affect how fast you can travel.

Once you're hiking, be aware of route-finding cues: Social trails can often veer off the main trail, heading to a viewpoint or campsite, and you can accidentally walk onto them without even noticing you're off the main route. Before you cross a stream, do you see where the trail picks up on the other side? When trails end at rock slabs or scree fields, don't assume that they just keep heading in the direction you were walking. Look for cairns—stacks of rocks that indicate the direction of travel—to guide you to the route. If you don't see cairns, look for other signs: Is there a worn section across the rock slab, or a line of rocks that looks more compacted than the rest of the scree? If you're not paying attention, it's easier than you might think to walk off the trail without even noticing.

PACE

Getting to the top of a mountain is never a race, and if you can learn anything from big-mountain climbers and guides, it's that pace is crucial. If you start out as fast as you can from the trailhead, you're not going to be able to keep up that pace all day. Repetitively going hard and fast for a short amount of time, then taking a break, then starting again is both physically and mentally exhausting.

Climbers slowly plod up the final steps to the summit of California's Mt. Shasta.

Think of the mountain as a city street with stoplights every block. Hiking at a good pace that pushes you, but not too much, is like driving at a moderate speed and hitting every light when it's green. Hiking fast, getting out of breath, stopping to catch your breath, then hiking fast again is like driving fast but getting a red light at every intersection. It's frustrating, harder on your car, and terrible for your gas mileage.

Your pace will slow as you hit steeper sections and/or when you get to higher altitudes. Don't worry about going too slow; just concentrate on moving. Even if you're only taking fifty steps each minute, you're still moving faster than if you have to stop every 2 minutes to lean on your trekking poles and catch your breath for 30 seconds.

Throughout a day of hiking, you'll take thousands of steps and obviously expend a significant amount of energy. You might not think that conserving energy makes any sense—the whole idea is to exercise, right? But using your energy in the right way can make a long day in the mountains a little less strenuous. "The First Rule of Mountaineering" goes: "Never stand when you can sit, and never sit when you can lie down." This idea is, of course, more appropriate for long, multiday trips (you're probably not going to do a lot of lying down during most day hikes), but the idea of conserving energy is there.

One technique to insert micro-rests into your hike or climb is a technique called the "rest step," a longtime mountaineering standby. On steeper terrain, your leg muscles will get a huge workout, moving almost nonstop for a long time. The rest step gives your muscles a tiny break every time you step, decreasing your level of fatigue—and it's ridiculously simple: When walking uphill, simply straighten your forward leg completely at the top of each step, just for a half-second. This gives your legs a small break with every step, putting your body weight on your skeleton instead of your muscles.

SELF-CARE

Over the course of a full day or multiple days of climbing a peak, you put your body through a lot—to make it to the top and back down again, you've got to take care of your body too.

Hydration

As with any strenuous exercise, peak bagging requires lots of water, especially at high altitude. By paying attention to when you're too hot and taking a jacket off before you start pouring sweat, you can help manage how much water you need on a peak climb. If you spend the first 2 hours of your hike dripping sweat out of every pore, you're obviously going to have to replace that fluid. So be mindful of when you're starting to get warm and, when possible, take a few seconds to remove a layer or two so that you can stay relatively cool. At altitude your body will require more water than usual, and not drinking enough can lead to altitude sickness, so pack a little extra water if you're heading above 10,000 feet. Your body may require more or less water than your hiking partners'—get to know your personal needs. Friends of mine have shown up for summit hikes to above 14,000 feet with only a single 20-ounce bottle of water, when I've needed 2.5 liters for the same hike.

How you hydrate is up to you. It's easier to drink small amounts more often with a hydration bladder, because you don't have to stop and open your pack every time you want to take a drink. Some hikers carry a running water bottle, take sips out of it as they hike, and then refill it from other bottles in their pack when they take a break.

If you sweat a lot, or have a hard time convincing yourself to drink water, consider adding an electrolyte or sports drink mix to your water—the taste can be a good incentive to drink more. Be aware, though, that your body may not be used to drinking multiple liters of sports drinks while exercising and might have a hard time processing the sugars in full-strength sports drinks. Water it down, or use a low-calorie mix.

Food

One of the great things about spending all day moving in the mountains is the amount of calories you burn—the reward being that you can replace a lot of calories on your way up and down by eating all kinds of tasty foods. There are myriad energy bar companies making a plethora of options for trail food, but remember that you're not limited to that aisle of the grocery store when you're shopping for a hike or climb. Experienced mountain guides tell clients, "Eat what you like," meaning bring foods you know you will eat, even when you're exhausted and your appetite is sapped from being at higher altitudes. Look in a guide's pack and you won't see a bag of energy bars. They'll often bring leftover Chinese food, cold pizza, chocolate bars, smoked salmon, and other snacks that make any energy bar flavor seem dull. One of my favorite tricks for a summit hike is to buy a burrito

A few hundred calories for a long day hike

from the freezer section at the grocery store and let it thaw in the top of my pack as I hike (of course all the frozen burritos are precooked). By the time I get to the summit, the burrito is soft enough to eat.

Here are a few important things to remember when packing food for a hike:

Provided you've had a solid meal before you start, you only need around 100 calories per hour while hiking to avoid "bonking" (sudden fatigue or loss of energy), and that can come from sports drink mixes, energy gels, "real food," or a combination.

You need a mix of protein, carbohydrates, and fat while hiking. If you try to complete a 12-mile summit hike on nothing but three bags of M&Ms, you might not feel so good at the top.

You're carrying all your food, so it's generally good to look for foods with a high calorie-to-weight ratio. Although it's healthy to eat lots of fruits and vegetables on a daily basis, you probably don't want to carry a grapefruit to the summit—it's quite heavy for something that only provides 100 calories, especially when you compare it with a 2-ounce Snickers bar that provides 250 calories. Nuts, cheese, jerky, crackers, dried fruit, hard-boiled eggs, and sandwiches all make great hiking food.

Skin

Skin receives a lot of collateral damage from peak bagging, mostly from blisters and sunburns. Well-fitting hiking shoes are the best way to avoid blisters, but if you haven't quite dialed in your shoes yet, pay attention when you feel "hot spots" forming on your feet. Carry a blister remedy like Second Skin or moleskin to combat hot spots before they become a show-stopper.

Sunburn can surprise you in the mountains—you're probably at higher altitude and closer to the sun, but the cooler mountain climate might prevent you from feeling the sun exposure. Be aware that you're at a higher risk of getting burned, and be sure to reapply sunscreen often. If you burn easily, consider wearing a sunhat or neck gaiter to keep the sun off your face and neck.

Windburn is also a consideration in areas exposed to wind. Sunscreen provides a small amount of protection, but if you're particularly sensitive, consider using a product like Vaseline or pull a neck gaiter over your face when it gets windy.

Chapter Seven

Scrambling

At some point on many peaks, the angle of the terrain will increase to a level where you have to start using your hands as well as your feet. Scrambling is one of the most fun parts of peak bagging for many people—travel becomes three-dimensional as you climb up, over, and around boulders, and routefinding becomes more interesting. The mountain can feel like a giant playground.

In the 1930s the Sierra Club developed a rating system to describe mountain travel. This eventually became known as the Yosemite Decimal System, which divides hikes and climbs into five classes. The exact definitions of each class are often debated, but generally follow these descriptions:

Class 1: Walking.

Class 2: Elementary scrambling, possibly requiring use of the hands.

Class 3: Scrambling with exposure, with use of hands mandatory.

Class 4: Simple climbing with more serious exposure (fatal falls are possible). Some parties may use a rope.

Class 5: Technical rock climbing requiring use of a rope, belaying techniques, and protection hardware.

A climber descends the southwest couloir of the Middle Teton, Grand Teton National Park, Wyoming.

The class rating of a route is a bit subjective, so take numbers with a grain of salt. One person's Class 3 can be another person's Class 4, and vice versa. A route rating helps you know in advance what to expect and what to bring. For example, if a route is Class 1, you might wear trail running shoes; for a Class 3 you might want approach shoes; and if it's Class 4, you might want a rope and a helmet.

Scrambling is a very intuitive method of travel and doesn't require advanced techniques—just a few things to focus on while you're doing it.

First and foremost, when you're in a boulder field or talus slope, always remember that a mountain is a pile of rocks, and some rocks are more stable than others. This saying from Colorado mountaineer and guidebook author Gerry Roach is a good one to remember: "Geologic time includes now." Aron Ralston, who was trapped behind a boulder for nine days in Utah's Blue John Canyon after the rock shifted when he moved over it, chose that quote for the first chapter of his memoir of the experience. What it means is that just because a rock has been in that spot for thousands (or millions) of years, it won't necessarily stay in that spot when you step on it.

When you're scrambling up a ridge or through talus, remember that quote; move with awareness and caution. Test handholds before you pull on them, and step on rocks gently at first, before you put all your weight on them. Boulder fields can be largely stable, all things considered, but you shouldn't recklessly bound up or down them assuming everything is solid and will stay that way for a thousand years (because it won't). As you gain more scrambling experience, you'll develop intuition and be able to read talus more easily and learn how to move more quickly, but still with caution.

A climber walks up the slabby approach to one northeast face of Vestal Peak in Colorado.

USE YOUR FEET, NOT YOUR HANDS

Any experienced rock climber will tell you that rock climbing is not about whether you can do a tremendous amount of pull-ups but whether you know how to use your feet. The same is true when you're scrambling. Your leg muscles are far bigger than your arm muscles and can support your body weight for much longer than your hands can—even on small footholds.

STAY IN BALANCE

It's not tightrope walking, but scrambling requires its own special type of balance. You're moving over uneven surfaces, and your feet are often situated at unique angles. Keep three points of contact when you're moving (two hands, one foot; or one hand, two feet), and if a rock moves out from under your hand or rolls out from under one of your feet, you'll be able to stay upright.

TIGHTEN UP

If you're carrying trekking poles and need to use your hands, collapse the poles and stow them on your pack to keep them out of the way. If you've got items strapped to the outside of your pack, get them packed away inside the pack and cinch down the straps to keep it as tight to you as possible. It's unnerving to snag a loose jacket or drop a water bottle as you're trying to climb up talus, and it's way easier to keep your balance if your pack feels like part of you instead of a heavy object pulling you backward or sideways.

STAY CALM

On some peaks, you might find yourself in what feels like an unstable situation or risking what feels like a dangerous fall. If you remain calm, you remain in control of the situation. Focus on what you need to do to move past the unstable or dangerous part—it's often a single move or step. Take your time and do what you need to do, whether that's making the move,

A climber picks out a safe route on Colorado's Notchtop Mountain.

finding another way around the section in question, or taking stock of the situation and deciding to back off and head back down the mountain.

LOOK OUT BELOW

When you're scrambling with a friend or above or below another party, be aware of where you are in relation to them, and always be careful moving through rock sections when they're above or below you. Once a rock starts rolling down a steep slope, it doesn't usually stop, and it usually takes a pretty erratic path downhill, bouncing and ricocheting off other rocks, making it very hard to dodge if you should find yourself in its path.

If you and a friend are scrambling together, stay out of the fall line of loose rocks as much as you can. You can do this by "switchbacking" up a talus slope, or choosing lines to the left or right of each other. If that's not possible (for instance, if you're climbing up a narrow gully), stay close enough to each other that a loose rock won't have a chance to gather much speed on its way down. If you're below your friend, keep your hands near the level of his or her feet and try to maintain the same pace. A loose rock falling onto you from 2 feet above is much less dangerous than one falling onto you from 20 feet.

A crowded day on the Trough on Longs Peak, Colorado

WHAT GOES UP MUST COME DOWN

Every year in Colorado's Garden of the Gods park, someone has to be rescued off the rock formations despite the signs warning visitors not to climb unless they have proper equipment. Typically the person has scrambled up some easy rock to a place where he or she was uncomfortable going any higher and then turned around, only to feel even more uncomfortable trying to reverse those steps. It's easy to

A hiker near the summit of Estes Cone in Colorado

find yourself in a similar predicament. Remember as you're scrambling up a section that you'll usually have to climb down it. If you're nervous about making the moves upward, it will be way more difficult making them on the way down.

Downclimbing is generally more difficult (and a little scarier) for most people, sometimes because it's harder to see handholds and footholds but often because we try to do it backward. It seems safer to slide down something on our butts instead of climbing down it facing the rock, but this is almost always wrong. If you lose your footing and you're butt-sliding and facing away from the rock, your hands are out in front of you where they can't help and your feet are also facing the wrong way.

When you encounter a difficult section of downclimbing, turn and face into the rock, and take as much time as you need to downclimb it safely. The difficult/scary part is often just a few feet between easier sections and can often require only a couple moves. Grab two good handholds, look for footholds below you, and try to make short moves instead of huge downward steps. Keep three points of contact, slowly lower yourself down, and never assume that jumping a few feet down would be easier.

Downclimbing is a necessary skill in the mountains. It can be a little scary at first, but if you stay calm and practice doing it correctly, it will become easier.

Chapter Eight
Basic Snow Travel

If you climb enough mountains, you're going to encounter snow at some point. For the purposes of this book, we'll cover basic snow travel and won't get into crevasse navigation and rescue or avalanche safety. If your objectives in the mountains include glacier travel, ice climbing, or climbing when avalanches are a major consideration (late fall through early spring), seek out further instruction from professional guides. We'll talk here about how to travel over the occasional snowfield, and be safe about it.

A small snow patch is generally no cause for alarm in the mountains, but when you encounter it, consider the following hazards:

» If you fall, where will you end up? Is it low-angled enough that you'll just fall down and be a little embarrassed? Or is it steep enough to send you downhill, fast and out of control, ending in a pile of boulders at the bottom or, worse, off a cliff?

» How deep is the snow? Generally, on most common mountain routes, by late spring, summer, and fall, snow should be consolidated enough that you can walk across it without sinking up to your hips, but conditions vary, and can vary even within a small patch of snow—

A climber heads up the Cristo Couloir on Colorado's Quandary Peak with her ice ax in her uphill hand.

as anyone who's surprisingly postholed up to his or her knee can tell you.

» What's underneath? Is the snow over a running creek, or a boulder field with lots of gaps between large rocks? You need to answer the question of what will happen if your foot punches through the snow. If you can't answer that, you need to decide whether it's safe to cross or not.

» What's the consistency of the snow? There's a big difference between trying to climb a steep pitch of wet slush sitting in the sun on a July afternoon and crossing a shady, north-facing patch of consolidated snow that you can kick steps into.

USING AN ICE AX

If where you're traveling has danger of a fall on snow (if the snow patch is steep and/or icy), or even the possibility of a fall on snow, you should have an ice ax with you and know how to use it. It's far better to carry an ice ax on your pack the entire day and never have to use it than it is to try to cross a sketchy snow-field with only a pair of trekking poles (or, even more desperate, a pair of pointy rocks you've picked up).

The ice ax is a very simple but useful mountaineering tool with five main parts:

1. The spike—the point at the bottom
2. The shaft
3. The head, or the top, which includes:
4. The adze—the flat, broad blade that's parallel to the ground when you hold the ax with the point facing down
5. The pick—the curved, toothed point opposite the adze

Ice ax parts: (1) spike, (2) shaft, (3) head, (4) adze, and (5) pick

Memorizing the names of these parts is not important, but knowing how to use them is. The first thing you should know how to do with an ice ax is how to stow it—because that's the first thing you'll do with it on a climb.

Your backpack will have an ice ax loop (or two) on the back, near the bottom of the pack. Take the spike of your ax and point it through the loop, with the pick pointed toward the middle of the back of the pack. Run the shaft of the ax through the loop, going away from the top of the pack. When you've slid the entire shaft through and the head of the ax is touching the loop, flip the entire ax over so that the spike is at the top and the loop is wrapped around the head of the ax. Secure the shaft against the pack with another strap, and you're ready to travel. If the ice ax

Attaching an ice ax to a day pack (clockwise from top left): point spike through ice ax loop; strap shaft to pack; properly attached ice ax

loop on your pack seems loose when you've got the ax stowed, simply twist the head around several times until the loop is tight, just before you strap the shaft to the pack. You now have a sharp, pointy object sticking out of your pack, so be careful when taking your pack out of your car, putting it on around your friends, and passing other hikers on the trail. The spike is at face height for most people, and it's no fun to be on the end of an accidental jab from someone's pack.

WALKING

The most obvious use for an ice ax is as a walking stick as you cross snow—this is very straightforward. When you use your ax as a walking stick, always have the adze pointing forward and the pick pointing backward.

A climber ascends a snowfield on the south side of the Middle Teton, Grand Teton National Park, Wyoming, using his ice ax as a walking stick.

SELF-BELAY

On steeper slopes, you'll use the ice ax as a self-belay so that it will catch you in case you slip. Carry the ax in your uphill hand, and as you step up, jam the spike of the ax into the snow above you, parallel to the position of your torso. Don't daintily push the spike into the snow—pop it down into the snow like you mean it. Imagine falling, and how secure the ax will need to be to hold your weight. Having the spike only 3 inches into the snow isn't going to do too much to help you. If you slip, hang on with the hand you're carrying the ax in, grab the shaft with your other hand, and hang on.

SELF-ARREST

If you should fall on a snow slope, the ice ax is your best friend. As soon as you feel yourself falling, get the pick into the snow as quickly and as securely as possible. In the ideal situation—falling facing the snow with your feet downhill—you will bring your fist holding the head of the ice ax up to chest height, grab the shaft near the bottom with your other hand so the ax is diagonal across your upper body, and press the pick into the snow with all your weight, leaning on it with your chest and shoulder. Dig into the snow as much as you can with your toes, kicking if necessary. If you're wearing crampons, you'll dig in with your

Practicing ice ax self-arrest BRETT SIMPSON

knees instead of your toes, because catching crampon points on snow while moving can cause injury or
flip you over.

There are, of course, other, non-ideal, ways of
falling, such as facing away from the snow or with
your head downhill. It might be hard to react in the
moment, but you have to fight to do four things: (1)
Get both hands on the ax, (2) get your pick into the
snow, (3) get your feet downhill, and (4) get your
face into the snow.

A NOTE ABOUT "STICKING THE LANDING"

Self-arrest is the first thing we are all taught about
using an ice ax, but there's something even more
important: not falling in the first place. A friend says
he always tells himself, "There's no such thing as a

self-arrest—you really have to stick the landing," which keeps him in the mindset of not falling. Pay attention to each step, and make sure your feet and crampons are always secure as you walk. The truth is, self-arrest is difficult, especially if you fall and gain significant speed as you slide down the snow. The best defense, in all cases, is to not fall and to never have to self-arrest—but you should practice and know how in case you ever need to do it.

TO LEASH OR NOT TO LEASH

There are several schools of thought on whether or not to attach an ice ax to a person: Some say it's foolish to not have it tied onto you, because if you drop it, you're in a very bad situation as you watch it slide away down the mountain. Others say it's a bad idea to have a sharp object attached to you if you fall, because if you lose your grip on it, you will have a very dangerous, pointy thing bouncing around next to you. I have used a leash and not used a leash

A climber with an ice ax leash attached to his waist

equally, and I personally prefer no leash in most cases. If I am using a leash, I prefer to attach it to my harness, not my wrist, so that when I'm changing directions or switchbacking up a slope, I don't have to detach and reattach it every time I want to switch hands. What you do is, of course, up to you.

STOWING BETWEEN SNOW SECTIONS

If you need to use both hands to scramble a short section of rock, or you have a short break between snowy sections where you don't need your ice ax, you don't have to fully stow it. Simply lift the ax above your head and slide the spike down between your backpack shoulder straps, with the adze over one shoulder and the pick over the other, and run the spike down your back (be careful if you're wearing a jacket with a hood) until the adze and pick are resting on your shoulder straps. When you need to use it again, pull it out by the head. This method isn't incredibly comfortable for miles and miles of hiking, but it works great for short sections.

GOING UP

To climb snow, you need to know a few simple techniques and points:

Always keep your ax in your "uphill" hand when traversing or climbing diagonally. When climbing

A climber on a winter climb of Colorado's Drift Peak

straight uphill, there is no uphill hand, so carry the ax in whichever hand is comfortable.

The snow on most common late spring–summer–early fall mountain climbs should usually be consolidated; depending on temperature, it will be either soft enough to kick steps in or hard enough to require crampons. If the snow is too hard to kick steps in and is steep enough that falling is a possibility, don't try to tough it out—take the time to put on your crampons.

When you're the first climber in a party, kicking steps is your job, and it's important to do it well. Don't worry about speed; worry about making a solid path for everyone in your party. When climbing, kick steps that you can get a good half-boot into, ensuring that everyone in your party will be able to climb securely. Kick at an angle slightly into the slope, making an upward-tilting step instead of downward-tilting. If other parties follow you up, kicking too-small steps doesn't help anyone. Once feet start slipping out of steps or breaking them, it doesn't take too long for the whole path—which you might have to use on your way down—to become a mess.

When snow is harder and kicking steps is strenuous, regularly switch out with other members in your party when possible so that one person is not doing all the work.

CRAMPONS

Sometimes on a climb, you'll encounter snow that's firm enough to warrant the use of crampons. During spring, summer, and early fall, it's often advantageous to get on a snow slope very early in the morning, because later in the day it becomes a soft, unclimbable slush patch. Depending on temperature and aspect, the snow can be steep enough and frozen enough that you'll want crampons on your feet.

Before you ever walk in crampons, they should be fitted to your mountaineering boots. When buying or renting crampons, take your boots into the store and make sure you're getting the proper model for your boots. Strap-on crampons will work with any boot, but step-in crampons will only work with boots with a welt on the heel and toe. While you're at the shop, size the crampons to fit your boots, and make sure they're snug at the heel and toe. Leave them sized for your boots when you put them away—it's no fun to get to the base of a snowfield when it's cold and dark and all of a sudden remember you have to resize your crampons for your boots.

It's fine to strap crampons to the outside of your pack, but make sure they're secure. Better yet, purchase a puncture-proof crampon bag for them. They're handy, and you can shove your crampons inside your pack, where they won't fall off.

Walking in crampons is fairly straightforward. Often the biggest issue is doing it well enough that you don't catch the sharp points on your pants—not just because they'll rip your expensive pants but because catching a crampon point on your pants at the wrong time can throw you off balance and send you tumbling down a slope.

When you encounter a snowfield that requires crampons, find a stable spot to stop and attach your crampons to your boots. I'm sure there are people who can stand on one foot and put a crampon on the other foot, but for most of us mortals, the best strategy is to find a rock to sit on. You don't want your day ending because you fell over trying to put on crampons.

There are four basic techniques for normal peak-bagging crampon use. They are, from not-so-steep to steep: normal walking, duckwalking, flat-footing, and front pointing.

On gentle slopes, you'll just walk normally. As the slope steepens, you can duckwalk, or walk with your toes pointing slightly outward and your heels in. The

Ascending the Mönch in Switzerland with crampons and ice ax

main point to remember is to keep as many points of your crampons in contact with the snow as possible, and to remain in balance while doing it.

Once a slope steepens to 30 to 45 degrees and duckwalking is uncomfortable for your ankles, you can use either flat-footing or front pointing.

Flat-footing is just how it sounds: You turn sideways, ice ax in your uphill hand, and step sideways up the slope, keeping as many crampon points on the slope as possible and avoiding edging with one side of your crampons or the other (hence "flat-footing"). Sidestep up the slope by crossing your downhill foot in front of your uphill foot, with your ice ax in the self-belay position. Only change the position of your ice ax when you're in the "in-balance" position (with

A climber frontpoints on Colorado's Apache Peak.

your legs uncrossed). Move deliberately and carefully, keeping your weight on your feet and concentrating on applying as much crampon to the slope as possible.

Front pointing is more strenuous and generally will be used sparingly on the level of climbs this book is intended for. As the name implies, front pointing is digging the front points of your crampons into the snow and stepping up—you can imagine that it's more strenuous, with all your weight supported by your toes. On most late spring–summer–early fall climbs, you'll likely use this technique sparingly, or on very short sections of hard snow.

If you're climbing longer sections of snow, visually inspect your crampons regularly during the climb to make sure the straps aren't coming loose and that the crampons remain secure on your boots.

COMING DOWN

There are three techniques for descending snow: downclimbing, plunge-stepping, and glissading. Descending snow can be a little scary at first, and you might feel that it is taking forever. That's OK—safety is the most important part, so take your time and concentrate on staying upright.

Downclimbing is the most secure (but slowest) way to descend: Face into the slope and kick steps or front-point down while keeping your ice ax in the self-belay position.

Plunge-stepping is a more confident move. On steeper slopes it can be a little hard to talk yourself into, but on soft snow it is a very quick way to descend. On your descent, the sun has typically risen higher and the air temperature has increased, warming the hard snow you climbed on your way up. To plunge-step down, hold your ice ax in one hand in the "walking stick" position (pick forward), face away from the slope, and step aggressively down on your heels. Take large downward steps, and remember that the more confidently you move down, the easier it will be.

Glissading is the fastest, most fun way to descend, but also the most dangerous. The biggest risk is losing control of a glissade and sliding at a high speed into obstacles below a snow slope, so be prudent and only try it where you determine it's safe. Don't glissade on hard snow, as you can lose control

A climber glissades down Queen's Way Couloir, Apache Peak, Colorado.

very quickly and it's very difficult to self-arrest. Never glissade with your crampons on, as they can catch and flip you over or injure your legs, feet, or knees. To glissade, sit down and hold your ice ax in the self-arrest position: top hand holding the top of the head of the ice ax with the pick on the pinky side of your hand and facing out from the chest; bottom hand holding the shaft, spike in the snow next to your hip, with the ax diagonal across your torso. Bend your knees and inch forward until you start sliding. Use the spike to control your speed as you slide; if you start to feel out of control, roll over to the spike side and self-arrest, driving your pick into the snow. Only glissade on slopes with enough snow to cover rocks beneath the snow or you'll have a not-so-fun ride down and possibly injure yourself. It's also possible to do a standing or crouching glissade by staying on your feet, which will keep your pants dry. This is a bit more advanced, but if you're a skier, you might find standing or crouching glissades quite intuitive.

Chapter Nine
Dealing with Altitude

In North America, especially in the West, plenty of the mountains we want to climb are at higher altitudes. Many of our famous peaks are above 10,000 feet: Mounts Rainier, Hood, Whitney, and Shasta and Longs Peak, to name a few. Altitude affects everyone, but it affects people differently—some people don't have major problems running ultramarathons above 10,000 feet, and some people get severe headaches while driving their car at 8,000 feet.

Atmospheric pressure is much lower at high altitudes than at lower altitudes, so using the term "thin air" is only somewhat scientifically correct. The air at 12,000 feet contains only 40 percent as much oxygen as the air at sea level, so you essentially have to take two and a half breaths to get the same amount of air as you get when you take a breath while standing next to the ocean.

Studies have shown that genetics play a significant part in whether someone gets altitude sickness, so if you get it once, you might likely get it again. However, that doesn't mean you'll always get it, or that you should give up climbing mountains. I personally have experienced dozens of mild (and some not-so-mild) episodes of altitude sickness when driving from Denver (elevation 5,280 feet) up to the mountains and then climbing peaks over 12,000 feet in the same day, but I had zero altitude problems during an eleven-day ridge traverse, during which I stayed above 10,000 feet for eight straight days.

PREVENTING ALTITUDE SICKNESS AND OPTIMIZING PERFORMANCE

Altitude sickness can be as simple as the slight discomfort of a headache and as severe as high-altitude pulmonary edema (HAPE), which can be fatal. HAPE is rare at altitudes of 14,000 feet and lower, but it can happen. If you're climbing peaks in the lower forty-eight and get altitude sickness, you most likely will experience acute mountain sickness (AMS), which is nonfatal but can progress to HAPE if not dealt with by descending or administering oxygen.

The symptoms of AMS are often compared to those of an alcohol hangover and include:

- » headache
- » lack of appetite
- » nausea
- » vomiting
- » dizziness
- » excessive flatulence

AMS is simply a collection of symptoms, meaning that if you have a headache at 11,000 feet, you're not necessarily going to experience nausea, vomiting,

A climber descends South Arapaho Peak in Colorado.

dizziness, and excessive flatulence too. Many people experience one or two symptoms at altitude with no further effects. For instance, someone who climbs several Colorado 14ers every summer might notice that she never feels like eating at high altitude, gets a mild headache on the summit, but never feels debilitated or seriously ill while climbing. On the other hand, someone who notices a headache at the trailhead at 10,000 feet and feels it getting worse as he ascends should be cautious (and maybe just turn around and come back another day). If the AMS symptoms worsen while you're hiking, it's no fun, and can be dangerous, to try to navigate down or up a mountain with a pounding headache, nausea, and dizziness. Anyone with worsening AMS symptoms should always turn around.

PREVENTING ALTITUDE SICKNESS

The number-one way to prevent altitude sickness (besides not going to high altitudes at all) is to ascend slowly. This can mean taking your time on the hike up to the summit during a one-day climb, or driving to the trailhead the night before and trying to "sleep high" before starting the climb the next morning. For instance, plenty of people are capable of doing the 4,800-foot-plus climb from the Longs

A climber near the summit of Apache Peak, Colorado

Peak Trailhead at 9,400 feet to the summit at 14,259 feet in a single day. But if you want to avoid altitude sickness symptoms, it's wiser to split the climb up into two days, hiking up to the Boulderfield (12,500 feet), camping for the night, and then heading to the summit the next morning.

Dehydration is another major cause of altitude sickness, and preventing it means not only staying hydrated on your climb but also making sure you start out well hydrated. What you do the day before your climb can affect your level of hydration as well, so keep that in mind before you have several beers the night before your climb and/or drink four cups of strong coffee on your way to the trailhead the morning of your summit hike.

Also make sure you're eating enough calories while ascending—altitude saps your appetite, so it's important to make yourself eat even if you don't feel hungry.

Even if you don't experience symptoms of AMS, the steps to prevent it—ascend slowly, stay hydrated, and eat well—can help you perform better at high altitude.

Chapter Ten

Overnighting in the Mountains

Single-day peak-bagging missions are fun and easy to plan: You grab some layers and a few snacks, drive to the trailhead, and start hiking. But there are a couple of reasons to extend a peak-bagging trip out overnight, or over several nights. As discussed in Chapter 9, breaking up a climb over two days can help you acclimate to higher altitudes. Making a backpacking trip out of a peak climb can also give you an extra day or two to attempt other objectives in the area, or you can make a "base camp" and spend several days climbing nearby peaks. Your reasons for overnighting can be as simple as seeing the sunset and sunrise from a backcountry campsite, or just getting away from your house for a couple days (and avoiding all that stuff that needs to be done around the house).

Having the skills and experience to backpack in to a climbing objective also increases your range. Plenty of summits are far enough in the backcountry to make them very difficult to climb in a single day, but if you're comfortable spending the night out, a two-day objective becomes possible. Climbing Mount Whitney via the Mount Whitney Trail, for instance, is a backbreaker of a day hike at 22 miles round-trip and 6,000 feet of elevation gain. It's far more pleasant as a two-day hike.

A climber rests during a three-day peak-bagging trip in Colorado's San Juan Mountains.

Camping adds an additional layer to the planning and packing process and means you have a heavier pack to carry, but it's worth the effort in a lot of ways. We won't get into the finer points of backpacking in this book (that's another book worth of material on its own), but we'll cover a few essentials for an overnight or multiday trip.

PLANNING

Not every summit hike makes for a good backpacking option. Some routes don't have great access to creeks or lakes for water resupplying, and some just don't have great campsite options. Sometimes camping is not allowed in a particular basin or drainage for

A selection of guidebooks

environmental reasons. Check around in guidebooks and on the Internet before you pick out a peak for an overnight trip. You don't want to have to walk an extra mile off the trail to get water to cook dinner and breakfast, or be unable to find a good place to pitch your tent and have to spend the night in a slanted, uncomfortable spot full of downed trees. Also find out if you need a permit to backpack in the area and, if you do, where you can obtain a permit. Does the area only permit three groups to camp in the backcountry in the same day? Do you need to apply in advance? Do you self-issue a permit at the trailhead? How much do permits cost? (You don't want to drive all the way to the trailhead and find out you don't have correct change to put in a permit envelope.)

Get a map of the area, and look for potential campsites near lakes and flat terrain near creeks.

FOOD STORAGE

Some backcountry areas require bear canisters for food storage, for the safety of both bears and humans.

Left to right: a bear canister, cord for a bear hang, and a stuff sack full of food for a bear hang

Find out beforehand if you need one. They're a bit bulky and cumbersome but very handy at the end of the evening, when all you have to do is stuff all your food in them and set them over by your "kitchen."

If bear canisters aren't required—and even if you're not camping in bear country—you'll likely still want to hang your food, so pack a large durable stuff sack and enough accessory cord to hang your food out of reach of bears (5 feet out from the trunk of a tree and 12 feet off the ground).

MAKE A PACKING LIST

Everyone's idea of what items are "necessary" on a backcountry trip is a little different. Here's a basic list of essentials for an overnight trip:

Sleeping:

Tent or tarp

Sleeping pad

Headlamp

Sleeping bag

Pillow (optional)

A hiker sets up a tent in Idaho's Sawtooth Mountains.

Kitchen:

Stove	Lighter and/or matches
Fuel	Pot or cook set
Bowl	Spoon or spork
Cup	Pocketknife and/or multitool

Bear canister or bear hang bag

Hydration:

Water bottles

Water treatment device or halogens

Food:

Dinner   Coffee   Breakfast   Snacks

Personal care:

Toiletries	Earplugs
Sunscreen	Insect repellent
Hand sanitizer	First-aid kit

Trowel for human waste disposal

Small repair kit (needle and thread, duct tape, patches for tent/sleeping pad)

Map and compass or GPS unit

WHAT SIZE PACK?

You'll also need to consider your pack—because you've got to carry everything in it. Generally, for a one-night, two-day trip, you should be able to get everything you need in a 45- to 50-liter backpack. For multiple nights out, you'll usually be carrying

A hiker with a pack carrying everything he needs for a three-day technical climb in Colorado's San Juan Mountains

the same items as for a one-night trip, adding more food and maybe a few additional clothing items, so you'll want a pack more in the 60- to 70-liter size. If you're buying your first backpacking pack, you might go with a bigger size. A 65-liter pack is usually only a few ounces—typically 6 or 8—heavier than a 50-liter pack, and it's more versatile in the long run, because you can use it for a three- or four-day trip as well as a one-night trip.

An additional consideration when buying a pack for overnight peak-bagging trips is what you're going to do when you leave camp and head for the summit. Do you want to haul your clunky 65-liter pack up the peak, even though you're just carrying food, water, and a few layers? Many pack manufacturers build packs with this in mind, making the lid removable with a fanny pack–style strap so you can take the lid off and use it as a small "summit pack." A different approach is buying an ultralight summit pack—they are usually inexpensive, add only 12 to 16 ounces to your pack weight, and are often more comfortable than a backpack lid.

If you're taking additional climbing gear, such as a helmet, crampons, or an ice ax, remember that you'll need to fit those items inside or attach them to your pack somewhere. Get complete packing, skills, and gear advice at backpacker.com.

Chapter Eleven

Going Light and Fast

Plenty has been said and written about traveling light in the backcountry: "Ounces equal pounds, and pounds equal pain." "Light is right." But probably the most accurate one is "The more you know, the less you need."

You can shop for ultralight gear and spend tons of money obsessively cutting ounces, but the best way to figure out how to go "light and fast" is by trial and error, and by periodically analyzing what's in your pack to decide whether you really need it. Over several years, I've personally trimmed down and gotten to a point where my pack is light but still includes everything I need for a safe outing in the mountains. For example, after a few years of hauling a bulky,

A climber carrying the bare essentials for an early morning summer solo climb of Utah's Mount Superior

extensive first-aid kit on every trip, I trimmed out a few things I never used, or wouldn't know how to use even if I needed them. I have never had a blister from boots or shoes (lucky me), so why should I carry a blister kit on every hike?

I also trimmed down some of my clothing, based on my experiences in the Mountain West. I realized that I always took a rain jacket and pants on every single hike but hardly ever wore rain pants. Either it never rained hard enough to talk myself into putting them on or I told myself I'd be OK hiking out and changing into dry pants at the trailhead. So I stopped packing rain pants, cutting a superfluous 10 to 12 ounces from every hike.

There are entire books and extensively researched websites about ultralight hiking and backpacking, and we can all learn a great deal about what's really necessary in backcountry travel from these resources. It's good to be prudent about your decisions and to be mindful about what others say is unnecessary. You'll develop your own systems and be able to test out whether they work for you or not. Certain things are essential in the backcountry. For example, 2 liters of water weigh about 4 pounds, and you wouldn't stop carrying water just because it's too heavy, would you? But maybe you don't need to carry a gallon of it for every day hike. And no one's going to tell me that 6 ounces of Starbucks Doubleshot is "unnecessary"—especially when I'm enjoying it on the summit.

Hikers on an extended hut-to-hut trip in the Italian Dolomites

Here's a guide with some basic day hiking and backpacking items to illustrate how much weight you can save with some small changes (the first item in each group is what's being replaced; the second item is the replacement; the third item is the weight difference):

Day Hiking

Hydration

Two 1-liter polycarbonate water bottles,
6.2 ounces each: 12.4 ounces
One collapsible 70-ounce polypropylene bottle:
1.3 ounces
Weight savings: 11.1 ounces

Feet

Men's hiking boots: 49 ounces per pair

Men's trail running shoes: 22 ounces per pair

Weight savings: 27 ounces

Trekking poles

Aluminum anti-shock trekking poles: 21.2 ounces

Carbon trekking poles: 18.2 ounces

Weight savings: 3 ounces

Backpack

25-liter daypack: 33 ounces

Ultralight 22-liter-capacity pack: 17 ounces

Weight savings: 16 ounces

Headlamp

Ultra-bright headlamp: 8 ounces

Ultralight headlamp: 2.4 ounces

Weight savings: 5.6 ounces

Rain gear

Rain jacket plus three-quarter-zip rain
pants: 27 ounces

Ultralight rain jacket: 7 ounces

Weight savings: 20 ounces

**Total weight savings: 82.7 ounces
(5 pounds, 2.7 ounces)**

Camping

Tent
Budget 2-person backpacking tent: 102 ounces
Ultralight 2-person backpacking tent: 48 ounces
Weight savings: 54 ounces

Sleeping pad
Basic backpacking sleeping pad: 30 ounces
Ultralight backpacking sleeping pad: 17 ounces
Weight savings: 13 ounces

Pillow
Camp pillow: 12 ounces
Extra clothes stuffed in stuff sack:
    no additional weight
Weight savings: 12 ounces

Cook set
Aluminum cook set: 26 ounces
Single titanium pot and lid: 8 ounces
Weight savings: 18 ounces

Water treatment
Pump water filter: 14.6 ounces
Iodine tablets: 3 ounces
Weight savings: 11.6 ounces

**Total weight savings: 108.6 ounces
(6 pounds, 12.6 ounces)**

Appendix A: Packing Lists

Day Hikes

Synthetic base layers

Pants or shorts

Socks

Shoes or boots

Gaiters (optional)

Rain jacket

Rain pants (optional)

Soft shell jacket

Puffy jacket (optional)

Sunhat (optional)

Beanie

Lightweight gloves

Trekking poles

Water bottles or hydration reservoir

Knife

Headlamp

First-aid kit

Navigation (map and compass and/or GPS)

Emergency kit

Water treatment items (optional)

Sunscreen

Personal locator beacon or satellite messenger (optional)

Ice ax (depending on climb)

Crampons (depending on climb)

Helmet (depending on climb)

Overnight Hikes

Sleeping:

Tent or tarp

Sleeping bag

Sleeping pad

Pillow (optional)

Headlamp

Kitchen:

Stove

Fuel

Lighter and/or matches

Pot or cook set

Spoon or spork

Bowl

Cup

Pocketknife and/or
multitool

Bear canister or bear
hang bag

Hydration:

Water bottles

Water treatment device
or halogens

Food:

Dinner

Breakfast

Coffee

Snacks

Personal care:

Toiletries

Earplugs

Sunscreen

Insect repellent

Trowel for human waste
disposal

Hand sanitizer

First-aid kit

Small repair kit (needle
and thread, duct
tape, patches for
tent/sleeping pad)

Map and compass or
GPS

Appendix B: Internet Resources

Backpacker.com
Backpacking gear reviews, outdoor skills information
and advice, and destinations for backpacking,
camping, and hiking.

SummitPost.org
User-submitted information and trip reports on
peaks throughout the US and the world.

14ers.com
User-submitted information and trip reports on
Colorado's 14,000-foot peaks.

13ers.com
A companion site to 14ers.com, covering Colorado's
13,000-foot peaks.

HighPointers.org
Official website of the Highpointers Club, a group
focusing on climbing the high points of each of
the fifty states.

HikeAZ.com
User-submitted information and trip reports for
Arizona hikes; includes dozens of peaks.

EveryTrail.com
User-submitted information for trails around the US.

CNYHiking.com
Website containing exhaustive information on hiking
in New York.